CROSS STITCH
DINOSAURS
and MONSTERS

Jane Greenoff

David & Charles

To my children, James Eric and Louise Estelle with love always

A DAVID & CHARLES BOOK

Copyright text, designs and charts © Jane Greenoff 1994
Copyright photographs © David & Charles 1994

First published 1994

Jane Greenoff has asserted her right to be identified as author of this work in accordance with the Copyright, Designs and Patents Act 1988.

A catalogue record for this book is available from the British Library.

ISBN 0 7153 0249 3

Typeset by ABM Typographics Ltd Hull
and printed in Italy
by LEGO SpA
for David & Charles
Brunel House Newton Abbot Devon

contents

how to stitch

Counted cross stitch is one of the easiest types of embroidery.

All the charted designs are made up of squares which you reproduce on your fabric as cross stitches. In the next section [page 6] you will see how to read a chart.

YOU WILL NEED

To work a design from this book you will need threads, Aida fabric 11 blocks to 2.5cm [1 inch] and a blunt tapestry needle, size 24 or 22.

Some stitchers like to use a hoop or frame when they are working cross stitch. It is not essential for this type of work.

All the designs in the book were worked without a frame.

THE THREADS

All the stitched designs in this book have been worked in stranded cottons (floss). Each length of thread is made up of six strands of cotton (floss) and you usually divide the strands before you start sewing.

All the cross stitch in this book is stitched using three strands of stranded cotton (floss).

It is a good idea to 'organise' your threads. Cut the threads into manageable lengths [50cm or 20 inches] and loop them on to a piece of punched card. This helps to stop tangles and knots.

THE FABRIC

All the designs in this book are stitched on 11 count Aida fabric. It is made of cotton and is specially woven for cross stitch. It looks as if it is made up of squares, which makes the counting much easier.

All the designs in the book are stitched from the centre of the fabric, which means you actually get the design in the middle. This is very important when you are ready to frame the finished piece.

The fabric used for cross stitch does tend to fray around the edges, so it is a good idea to neaten the edge in some way. Either fold over and stitch a narrow hem or oversew the edge loosely. This stitching can be pulled out when the work is finished.

HOW TO STITCH

Find the centre of the fabric, which is where you begin stitching. To do this, fold the fabric in half, then in half again and press lightly. Work a line of tacking (basting) stitches along the folds, as shown opposite. The lines meet at the centre, marking the position of the first stitch. (Remove the tacking carefully after the cross stitch design is finished.)

Divide the strands of cotton (floss) and thread your needle with three strands.

Look at picture A opposite. Bring the needle up at point 1 (but at the centre of the fabric).

Leave a short end on the wrong side [see picture B].

Cross the square and go down through point 2.

Come up again at point 3.

Cross the square and go down through point 4. Note the position of the needle. Repeat, to make a row of half crosses.

Complete the cross stitches as shown in C. As you work each cross stitch on the material, it matches one square on the chart.

To prevent the loose ends from undoing themselves, you will need to finish them off as you go. It is better not to use knots as they cause lumps and bumps that show on the front when the work is finished.

After working a few stitches, turn the work over to the wrong side and catch in the thread left at the start [see picture D].

When you have finished one colour, finish off the ends in the same way [see picture E].

Picture F shows that the top stitch should face the same way whether you are working up and down or from left to right.

Picture G illustrates how to add the backstitch outline around blocks of colour.

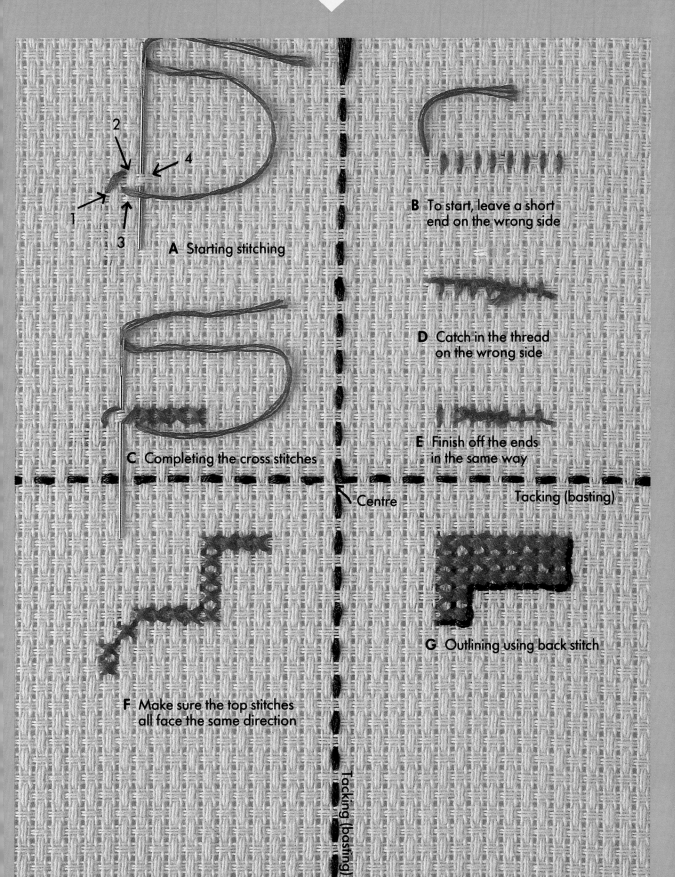

A Starting stitching

B To start, leave a short end on the wrong side

C Completing the cross stitches

D Catch in the thread on the wrong side

E Finish off the ends in the same way

Centre

Tacking (basting)

F Make sure the top stitches all face the same direction

G Outlining using back stitch

Tacking (basting)

how to read a chart

On the page opposite you will see a large coloured chart of the grumpy spider and his web.

This design is illustrated in the colour photograph on page 9. Full stitching instructions are on page 8.

The grumpy spider and web chart is drawn in felt-tip pens on squared paper.

Each square on the paper represents one square on your fabric. As we discovered in the picture on page 5, the Aida fabric used for all the stitching in this series of books is also made up of squares.

All the charts in the book are drawn in the same way. Each one has a key showing a list of thread colours used next to the symbols used on the chart. The grumpy spider design uses different shades of brown and honey, outlined in chestnut, and the web is stitched in black back stitch.

The central stitch is marked on the chart. You can see that the first stitch on the grumpy spider is blank, so you will need to work the stitch in the square to the right, which is chestnut. As with each project, the stitching instructions for the grumpy spider tell you where to start and in which direction to stitch. You will soon get the idea.

All the symbols are worked in cross stitch in the colours listed in the key. You can use any colour or brand of thread you like, but if you want to copy the design in the colour photograph exactly, you will need to use DMC stranded cottons (floss). The DMC shade numbers are included in each project, along with Anchor numbers for people who prefer to use Anchor threads.

The solid outlines around the stitching are worked in back stitch when the cross stitch has been completed [see pages 4 and 5]. You can see that the outline of the grumpy spider is stitched in chestnut.

notes for parents and teachers

Counted cross stitch is one of the simplest, least expensive and most rewarding types of needlecraft and is suitable for children of all ages and both sexes!

My own experience of teaching children under ten has been a revelation. The children concerned were all volunteers after school hours and were mostly boys. After learning the basic stitch, all the children were keen to stitch and design for themselves.

The most successful children were those whose first projects were small and quickly completed. They were therefore eager to experiment.

HOW TO HELP

1 Choose small projects with large blocks of colour.
2 Select fabric that can be seen clearly and handled easily.
   Aida fabric is available in 8, 11, 14, 16 and 18 blocks to 2.5cm [1 inch]. All projects in this book use 11 count Aida.
3 Use blunt tapestry needles with large eyes in size 24 or 22.
4 Be prepared to thread and re-thread needles to start with. You may find it helpful to have a number of threaded needles ready for use.

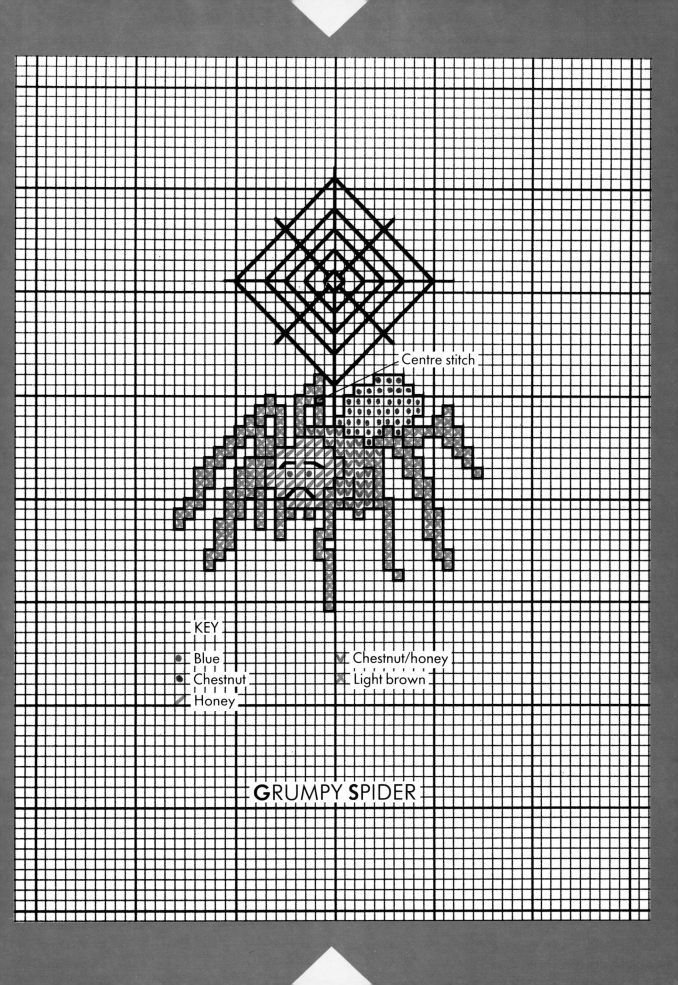

Centre stitch

KEY

● Blue   ✔ Chestnut/honey
● Chestnut   ✕ Light brown
╱ Honey

GRUMPY SPIDER

GRUMPY SPIDER

THREADS

COLOUR	DMC	ANCHOR
Blue	792	0177
Chestnut	433	0371
Honey	437	0362
Light brown	435	0901
Black	310	0403

STITCHING INSTRUCTIONS

● Cut a piece of Aida fabric not less than 15 x 18cm [6 x 7 inches] and hem the raw edges to prevent fraying [see page 4].

● Remember that all the projects in this book were stitched on 11 count Aida. This means that there are 11 stitches to 2.5cm [1 inch].

● Mark the centre of the fabric with lines of tacking stitches [see page 5].

● Thread your needle with three strands of chestnut stranded cotton (floss) and look at the chart on page 7. As the central marked stitch is blank, work the stitch in the square to the right in chestnut and, working towards the spider's bottom, keep the top stitch of each cross stitch facing in the same direction [see page 5]. To

make the work easier, you can turn it upside down and work towards the spider's legs, but remember to turn the chart the same way.

● Work all the chestnut shade, then start the top section of the spider's body. To do this, thread your needle with two strands of chestnut and one strand of honey together. This is a very simple way of altering the colour of your stitching although you are still using the same shades.

● Continue working all the cross stitches in the same way, finishing off the ends as you go [see page 5].

● When the cross stitch is complete, remove the tacking threads marking the centre, check for missed stitches and then add the outlining.

OUTLINING

● Thread your needle with two strands of chestnut stranded cotton (floss). Add the outline in back stitch, following the chart and working around the spider as shown in the photograph.

● Then add his grumpy mouth and eyebrows in back stitch on top of your cross stitch.

● Using two strands of black, stitch the web in back stitch.

Note: You can see different versions of the spider in the colour picture on pages 16 and 17.

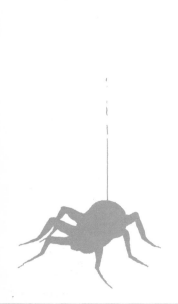

SPOTTED MONSTER

THREADS

COLOUR	DMC	ANCHOR
Bright blue	995	0410
Pink	335	041
Black	310	0403
Yellow	725	0306
Purple	327	0100
Green	937	0263

STITCHING INSTRUCTIONS

● Cut a piece of Aida fabric not less than 26 x 17cm [10 x 7 inches] and hem the raw edges to prevent fraying [see page 4].

● Mark the centre of the fabric with lines of tacking stitches [see page 5].

● Thread your needle with three strands of purple stranded cotton (floss), look at the chart and, starting from the marked central stitch, work across towards the monster's back leg and tail, remembering to keep the top stitch of each cross stitch facing in the same direction.

● When you have finished the purple areas, fill in the monster's spots in yellow. (If you would like to experiment, try different coloured spots!)

● Continue working all the cross stitches in the same way, finishing off the ends as you go [see page 5].

● To stitch the monster's eyes, thread your needle with three strands of dark blue and work one cross stitch for each eye.

● When the cross stitch is complete, remove the tacking threads marking the centre, check for missed stitches and then add the outlining.

OUTLINING

● Thread your needle with two strands of black stranded cotton (floss) and add the outline in back stitch [see page 5].

SPOTTED MONSTER

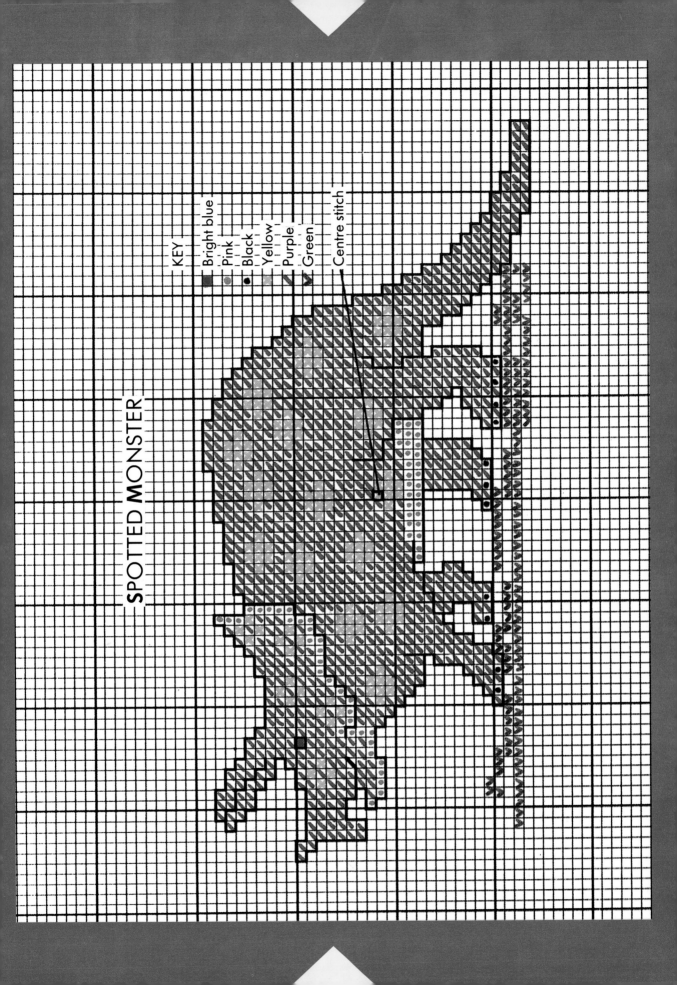

KEY

Bright blue
Pink
Black
Yellow
Purple
Green

Centre stitch

CROSS CROCODILE

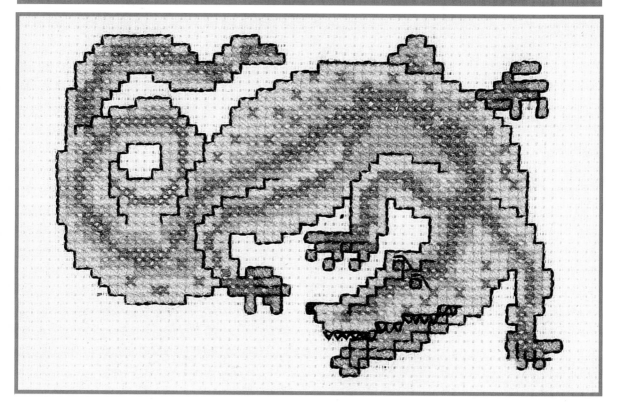

THREADS

COLOUR	DMC	ANCHOR
Pink	351	010
Blue	806	169
Stone	3032	0903
Dark brown	632	0936
Coffee	436	0363
Honey	738	0372
Black	310	0403

STITCHING INSTRUCTIONS

● Cut a piece of Aida fabric not less than 22 x 17cm [10 x 7 inches] and hem the raw edges to prevent fraying [see page 4].

● Mark the centre of the fabric with lines of tacking stitches [see page 5].

● Thread your needle with three strands of honey stranded cotton (floss), look at the chart and, starting from the marked central stitch, work towards the crocodile's front leg, keeping the top stitch of each cross stitch facing in the same direction.

● Using the dark brown, start working the stripe down the crocodile's back. You can decide in which direction you would like to work. The stripe goes from his nose to the tip of his tail!

● Continue working all the cross stitches in the same way, finishing off the ends as you go [see page 5].

● When the cross stitch is complete, remove the tacking threads marking the centre, check for missed stitches and then add the outlining.

OUTLINING

● Thread your needle with two strands of black stranded cotton (floss) and add the outline in back stitch.

● Outline all the large areas of colour first, then add the zig-zag lines to make the crocodile's teeth.

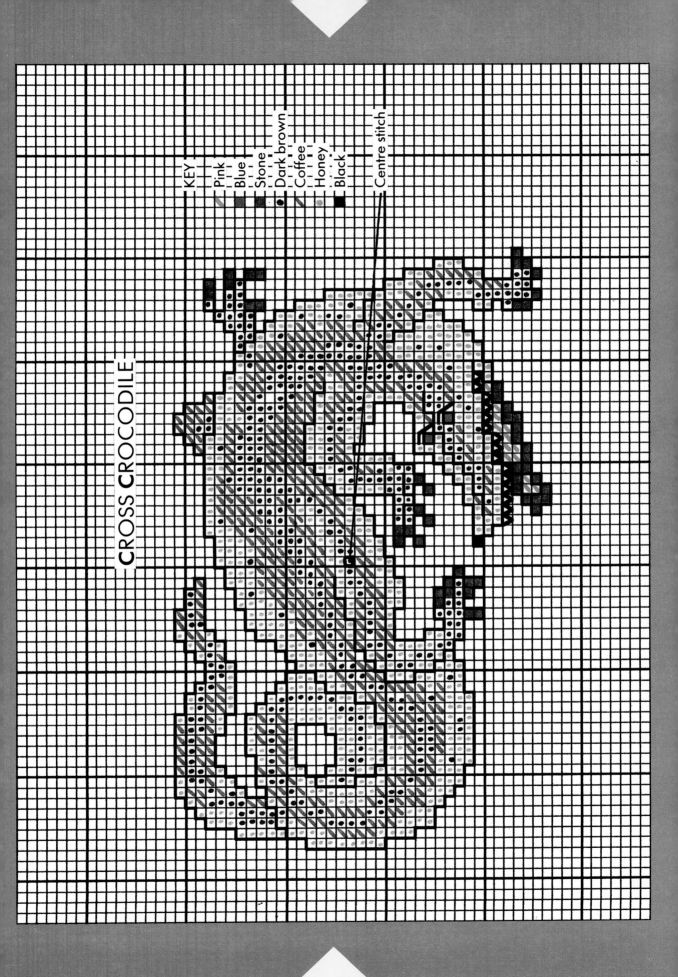

CROSS CROCODILE

KEY
Pink
Blue
Stone
Dark brown
Coffee
Honey
Black

Centre stitch

TERRIBLE T. REX

THREADS

COLOUR	DMC	ANCHOR
Red	349	013
Yellow	744	0301
Dark brown	898	0381
Black	310	0403
Dark grey	413	0401
Stone	612	0832
Green	562	0210

STITCHING INSTRUCTIONS

● Cut a piece of Aida fabric not less than 25 x 20cm [10 x 8 inches] and hem the raw edges to prevent fraying [see page 4].

● Mark the centre of the fabric with lines of tacking stitches [see page 5].

● Thread your needle with three strands of stone stranded cotton (floss), look at the chart and, starting from the marked central stitch, work from the middle down and towards T. rex's front leg, keeping the top stitch of each cross stitch facing in the same direction. You can choose which colour you work next.

● Continue working all the cross stitches in the same way, finishing off the ends as you go [see page 5].

● When the cross stitch is complete, remove the tacking threads marking the centre, check for missed stitches and then add the outlining.

OUTLINING

● Thread your needle with two strands of black stranded cotton (floss). Add the outline in back stitch around T. rex's body and the zig zag lines for his sharp teeth. Remember to add his angry eye in three strands of red!

● Note: Part of T. rex is used in Design a Dragon on page 26.

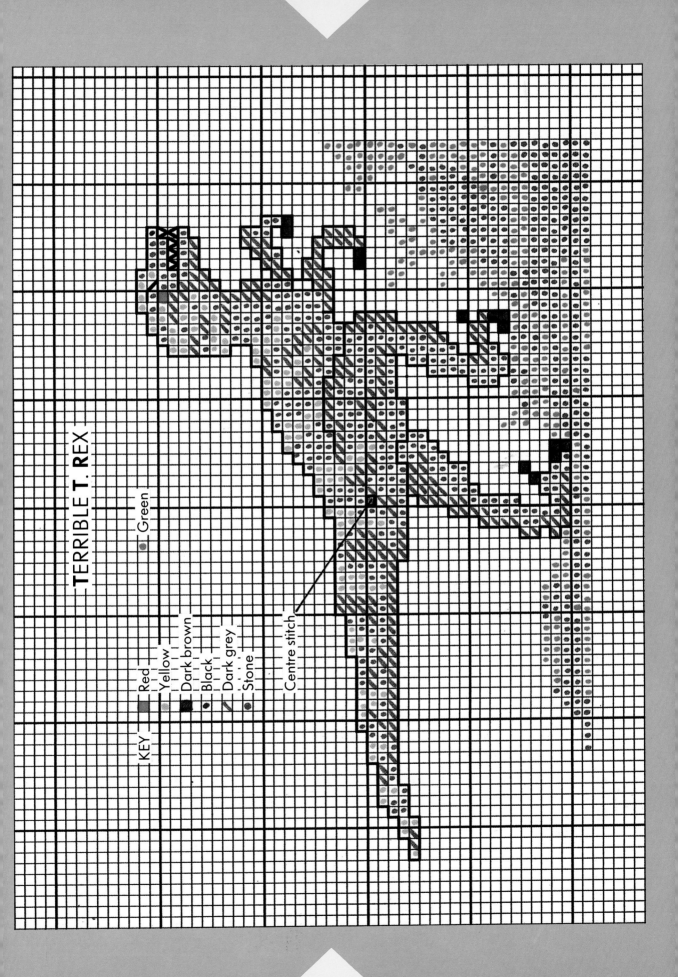

TERRIBLE T. REX

KEY

Red	
Yellow	
Dark brown	
Black	
Dark grey	
Stone	
Green	
Centre stitch	

HUNGRY DIPLO

HUNGRY DIPLO

KEY
- ● Purple
- ╱ Green
- ╱ Yellow
- ■ Black
- ● Darker green
- ● Blue
- ✕ Dark brown

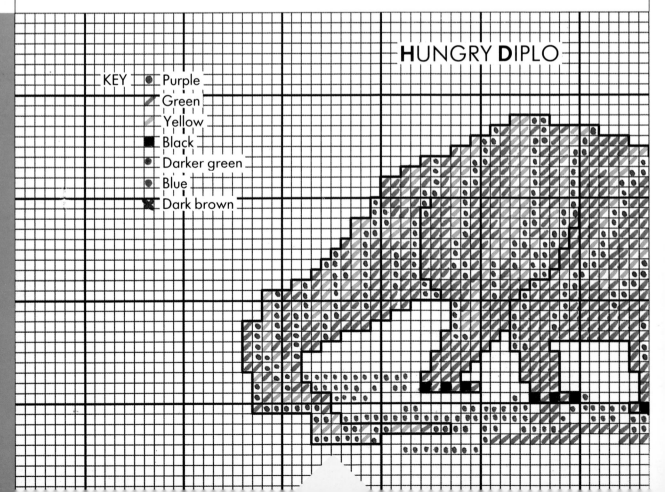

THREADS

COLOUR	DMC	ANCHOR
Purple	327	0100
Green	562	0210
Yellow	676	0891
Black	310	0403
Darker green	561	0212
Blue	792	0177
Dark brown	898	0381

STITCHING INSTRUCTIONS

● Cut a piece of Aida fabric not less than 32 x 20cm [13 x 8 inches] and hem the raw edges to prevent fraying [see page 4].

● Mark the centre of the fabric with lines of tacking stitches [see page 5].

● Thread your needle with three strands of green stranded cotton (floss), look at the chart and, starting from the marked central stitch, work across and down towards the diplo's tummy, keeping the top stitch of each cross stitch facing in the same direction.

● When you have finished this needleful, you can continue with the green or start working the diplo's stripes.

● When the diplo is complete, you can add as much grass as you wish.

● To work the tree, count down from the monster's neck and across to the tree trunk. It is always easier to count stitches than fabric squares.

● Continue working all the cross stitches in the same way, finishing off the ends as you go [see page 5].

● When the cross stitch is complete, remove the tacking threads marking the centre, check for missed stitches and then add the outlining.

OUTLINING

● Thread your needle with two strands of black stranded cotton (floss) and add the outline in back stitch around the hungry diplo. Don't forget to add his smile!

● Note: Part of the hungry diplo is used in Design a Dragon on page 26.

Centre stitch

NESSIE

THREADS

COLOUR	DMC	ANCHOR
Black	310	0403
Light blue	931	0921
Bright blue	792	0177
Light green	368	0214
Stone	3032	0903
Dark green	367	0216
White	blanc	01

● As no one knows what he or she looks like, perhaps you could stitch Nessie in tartan!

STITCHING INSTRUCTIONS

● Cut a piece of blue Aida fabric not less than 35 x 16cm [14 x 6 inches] and hem the raw edges to prevent fraying [see page 4].

● Mark the centre of the fabric with lines of tacking stitches [see page 5].

● Look at the chart and you will see that the middle square is blank, so you will need to count down to the bright blue squares and begin stitching here. Thread your needle with three strands of bright blue stranded cotton (floss), look at the chart and, starting from the marked central stitch, work across and down towards the water,

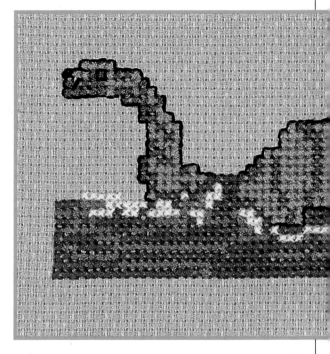

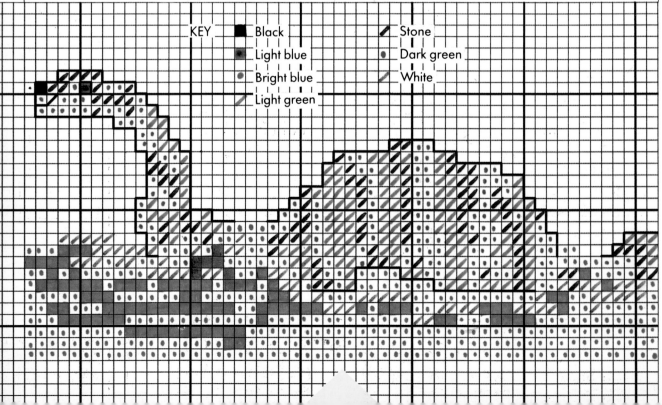

KEY
■ Black
● Light blue
● Bright blue
⁄ Light green
⁄ Stone
● Dark green
⁄ White

keeping the top stitch of each cross stitch facing in the same direction.

● Continue working all the cross stitches in the same way, finishing off the ends as you go [see page 5].

● When the cross stitch is complete, remove the tacking threads marking the centre, check for missed stitches and then add the outlining.

OUTLINING

● Thread your needle with two strands of black stranded cotton (floss) and add the outline in back stitch around Nessie's head and humps.

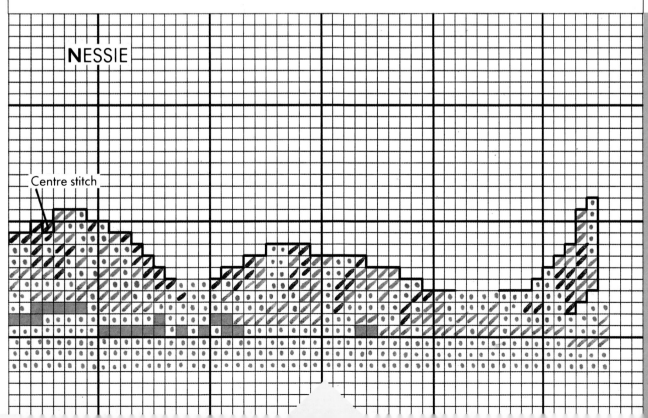

NESSIE

Centre stitch

STEALTHY STEGO

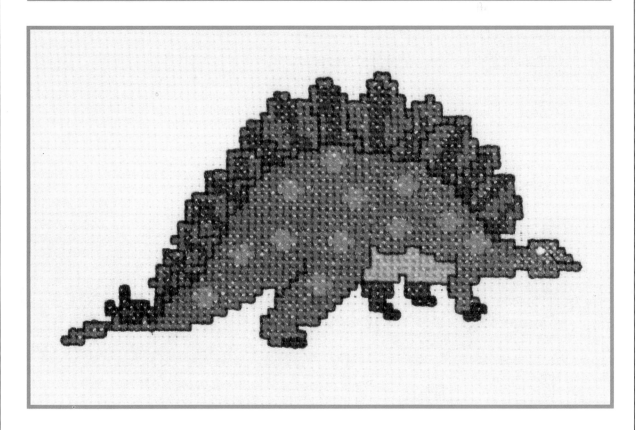

THREADS

COLOUR	DMC	ANCHOR
Green	562	0210
Orange	722	0323
Purple	327	0100
Dark brown	898	0381
Bright orange	721	0324

● The stego in the picture looks very creepy because his eye is left unstitched. You could add a yellow or red stitch to create different effects.

STITCHING INSTRUCTIONS

● Cut a piece of Aida fabric not less than 25 x 20cm [10 x 8 inches] and hem the raw edges to prevent fraying [see page 4].
● Mark the centre of the fabric with lines of tacking stitches [see page 5].

● Thread your needle with three strands of green stranded cotton (floss), look at the chart and, starting from the marked central stitch, work across and down towards the stego's back leg, keeping the top stitch of each cross stitch facing in the same direction.
● Continue working all the cross stitches in the same way, finishing off the ends as you go [see page 5].
● When the cross stitch is complete, remove the tacking threads marking the centre, check for missed stitches and then add the outlining.

OUTLINING

● Thread your needle with two strands of dark brown stranded cotton (floss) and add the outline in back stitch around the body.
● Using one strand of brown, add the smile, and, if you want more detail, the lines on his spines.

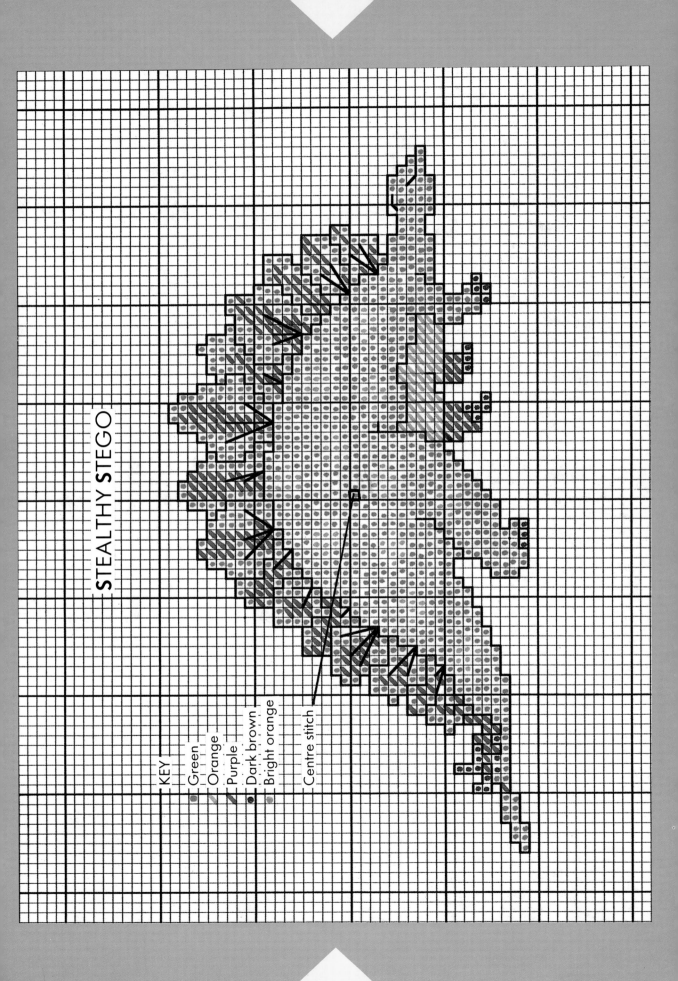

STEALTHY STEGO

KEY
- Green
- Orange
- Purple
- Dark brown
- Bright orange
- Centre stitch

SKULL

THREADS

COLOUR	DMC	ANCHOR
Dark grey	413	0401
Coffee	436	0363
Honey	738	0372

The skull is illustrated in the photograph on pages 16 and 17 and is stitched on bright red Aida fabric, which makes him look quite scary! The bat is stitched separately on dark blue Aida fabric to look like a night sky, but the two could be combined to make a very eerie picture. The skull could also be stitched on dark blue or black Aida fabric to achieve a different effect. Why not try changing the colours and see what happens?

To copy the skull exactly as illustrated in the photograph on pages 16 and 17, follow the instructions below.

STITCHING INSTRUCTIONS

Cut a piece of red Aida fabric 16 x 18cm [7 x 8 inches] and hem the raw edges to prevent fraying [see page 4].

Mark the centre of the fabric with lines of tacking stitches [see page 5].

Looking at the chart opposite, you will see that the marked central square is blank. Thread your needle with three strands of coffee stranded cotton (floss) and, looking at the chart, start stitching to the left of the nose, working across and down towards the skull's teeth and keeping the top stitch of each cross stitch facing in the same direction.

Continue working all the cross stitches in the same way, finishing off the ends as you go [see page 5].

When the cross stitch is complete, remove the tacking threads marking the centre, check for missed stitches and then add the outlining.

OUTLINING

Thread your needle with two strands of dark grey stranded cotton (floss) and add the outline in back stitch.

VAMPIRE BAT

THREADS

COLOUR	DMC	ANCHOR
Red	321	9046
Coffee	632	0936
Mushroom	407	0914
Dark honey	436	0363
Brown	435	0901

STITCHING INSTRUCTIONS

Cut a piece of dark blue Aida fabric not less than 13 x 13cm [5 x 5 inches] and hem the raw edges to prevent fraying [see page 4].

Mark the centre of the fabric with lines of tacking stitches [see page 5].

Thread your needle with three strands of mushroom stranded cotton (floss), look at the chart and, starting at the marked central stitch, begin stitching the bat's head, keeping the top stitch of each cross stitch facing in the same direction.

The detail of the bat's face is added by back stitching on top of your cross stitch.

continued overleaf

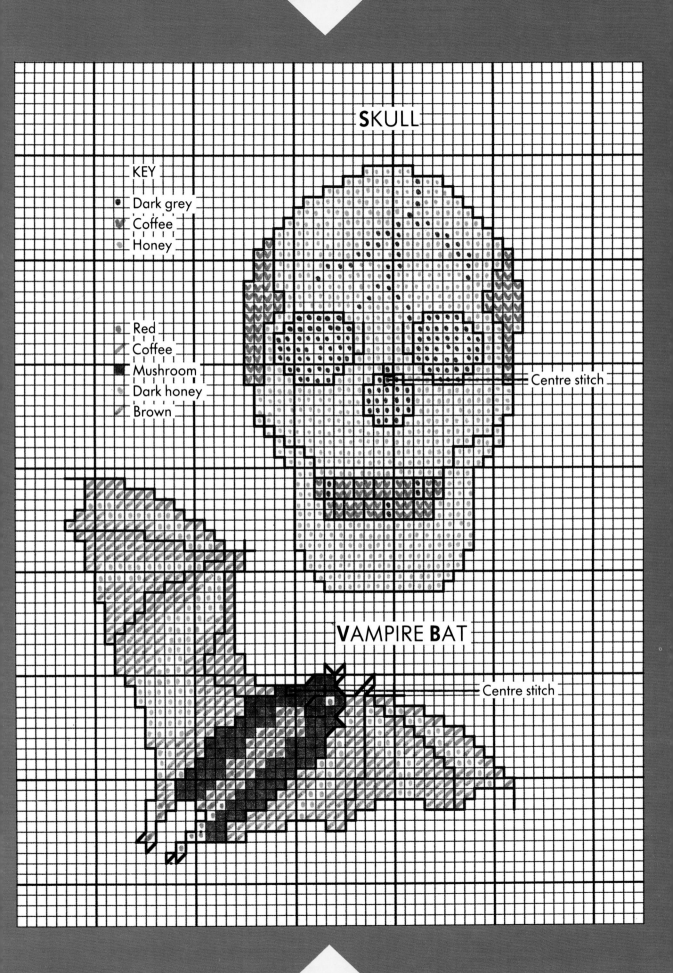

SKULL

KEY

- Dark grey
- Coffee
- Honey

- Red
- Coffee
- Mushroom
- Dark honey
- Brown

Centre stitch

VAMPIRE BAT

Centre stitch

Look at the chart and you will see that one colour is made up of two shades. When you work these stitches mix the colours on your needle by using two strands of dark honey and one strand of coffee.

Continue working all the cross stitches in the same way, finishing off the ends as you go [see page 5].

When all the cross stitch is complete, remove the tacking threads marking the centre, check for missed stitches and then add the outlining.

OUTLINING

Thread your needle with two strands of coffee stranded cotton (floss) and add the outline in back stitch.

design for yourself

This section and Project Ten are intended to give you the opportunity to design for yourself. The beauty of cross stitch is that you can alter designs to suit bigger projects by combining the patterns. You can see this with the dragon chart on pages 26 and 27, which is made from the body part of the hungry diplo and the head and tail from terrible T. rex.

HOW TO DESIGN

Using a soft pencil and squared paper, copy the outline of the designs you want.

Cut out the drawn shapes and move them around until you have a pleasing arrangement, then glue them to another sheet of squared paper and follow this new chart to stitch your own masterpiece!

Volcano valley at the front and back of the book was produced in the same way. The hungry diplo and stealthy stego are seen with volcano valley's terror-bird flying above their heads. The terror-bird, volcanoes, snow-capped mountains and greenery are charted on page 29.

It is not necessary to copy all the details from the charts because you can stitch your designs from the book when you have finished planning. The outline should be sufficient.

MEASUREMENTS AND COLOURS

If you make up your own designs, you will need to calculate the amount of fabric needed. For every 11 squares on the chart you will need 2.5cm [1 inch] of 11 count Aida fabric. Remember to add 10cm [4 inches] to both dimensions for the margins.

The colours and shade numbers included in this section are for your guidance. Why not try experimenting with different colours?

HAPPY DESIGNING!

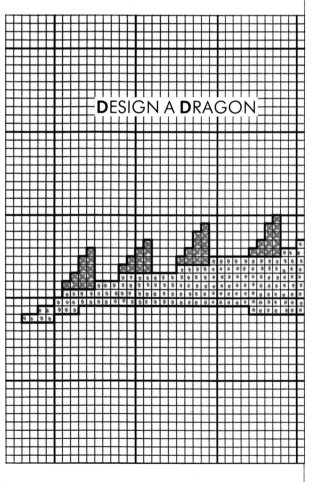

DESIGN A DRAGON

design a **d**ragon

This project can be great fun. The chart illustrates how easy it is to design for yourself. The dragon is made from the charts on pages 15 and 19, or you can make up your own version.

Draw the outlines of two of the monsters in the book using a soft pencil and squared paper, then cut them up into sections and fit them back together again! See if you can see which sections of the hungry diplo and terrible T. rex I have used in the chart.

Once you have an outline of your dragon, you can add spines, scales and fiery breath! The chart includes wings and some sharp spines to add the finishing touches.

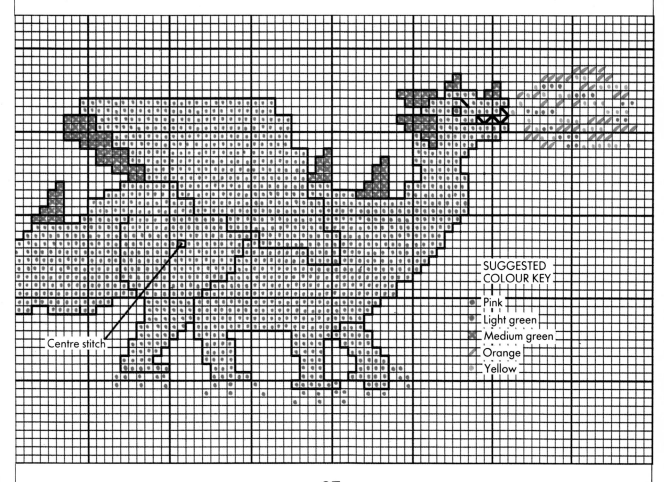

Centre stitch

SUGGESTED
COLOUR KEY

Pink
Light green
Medium green
Orange
Yellow

VOLCANO VALLEY

KEY
White
Red
Orange
Yellow
Stone
Dark brown
Purple
Light green
Dark green
Medium green
Dark grey
Light grey

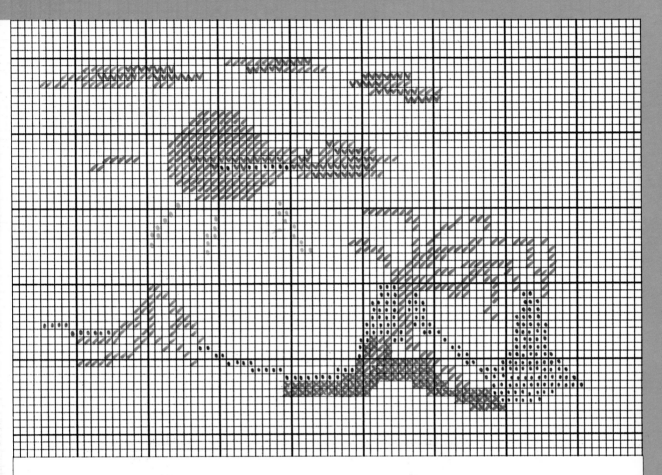

PROJECT TEN

VOLCANO VALLEY

THREADS

COLOUR	DMC	ANCHOR
White	Blanc	01
Red	600	078
Orange	722	0323
Yellow	725	0306
Stone	3032	0903
Dark brown	898	0398
Purple	327	0100
Light green	562	0210
Dark green	561	0216
Medium green	367	0214
Dark grey	413	0401
Light grey	3072	0274

Volcano valley is illustrated at the beginning and the end of the book and on pages 16 and 17. It is made up by combining the charts shown here with the charts for hungry diplo and stealthy stego.

To make a similar design, copy monster outlines from the book using a soft pencil and squared paper, cut them out and arrange them as described in Design for Yourself on page 26. Using crayons or felt-tip pens, copy or draw mountains and volcanoes to add an interesting background to your design.

The colours given for the terror-bird are suggestions, but you can try out your own ideas.

simple mounting and framing

When you have completed a cross stitch design you may wish to make the finished piece into a picture, perhaps to give as a gift.

In some cases a simple 'flexi' frame may be used. These are simple plastic frames made in two parts and the stitching is sandwiched between them. Needlework shops stock many different sizes and colours, so you can choose the best for your design.

If you would like to make your design into a card for a friend, there are dozens to choose from, so you can select the colour and shape of card to suit your stitching. (Follow the manufacturer's instructions.)

If you prefer to make your project into a picture with a rigid frame, you will need to stretch the material to remove any wrinkles and ensure that the stitching is straight! Before you start, wash the stitching if necessary and then iron it [see opposite].

It is not difficult to mount a piece of stitching yourself if you follow the instructions below.

MOUNTING INSTRUCTIONS

You will need:
- stiff card or foam core (available from picture framers)
- glass-headed pins
- double-sided sticky tape
- masking tape
- purchased frame
- scissors
- tape measure or ruler
- pencil

1 Work on a clean, flat surface.
2 Cut a piece of card or board that will fit your frame.
3 Measure the card along the bottom edge and mark the middle with a small pencil mark.
4 Repeat for all four sides.
5 Mark the middle of the bottom edge of the design with a pin and match the two centres.
6 Working from the middle, pin the fabric to the card as shown [see below].
7 Turn the work and pin the opposite side in the same way.
8 Turn to one side and pin from the centre as before.
9 You will then have pins all the way around the card [see below].
10 Check that the design is straight and that you have removed any wrinkles.
11 Turn the work over to the wrong side and, using double-sided sticky tape, stick down the excess fabric, one side at a time [see below].
12 Do not remove all the pins until all the sides are fixed in place.
13 Tape down the raw edges using masking tape and put the mounted stitching into the frame, then fix in position.

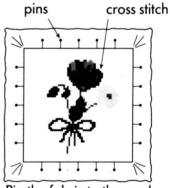

pins   cross stitch

Pin the fabric to the card
on all four sides

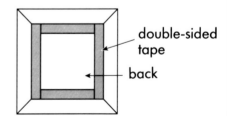

double-sided tape

back

Stick down the excess fabric

washing and ironing cross stitch

Here are a few simple tips to follow when you have finished a piece of cross stitch and wonder what to do next.

WASHING

Try to avoid washing your piece at all. Keep your stitching in a safe clean place, away from pets and worst of all, food and drink.

Even in the best-run homes accidents will happen, so it may be necessary to wash a piece of stitching. If you have used either of the brands of thread mentioned in the book, there is no danger of the colour running as long as you wash the item in warm water by hand. Allow the fabric to dry naturally and then press as below [do NOT use the tumble dryer].

IRONING

Before using a hot iron, check with an adult. Ask for help rather than burning your work or, worse still, yourself!

Heat the iron to a hot setting and use the steam button if your iron has one. Cover the ironing board with a THICK layer of towelling. I use four layers of bath towel.

Place the stitching on the towel, right side down, with the back of the work facing you. Press down on the piece firmly.

acknowledgements

I would like to thank all the people who made this book possible. My husband Bill, who continues to support me, often under impossible circumstances! My children James and Louise, who gave me the idea, and Vivienne Wells at David & Charles who still believes in me!
Michel Standley and all the Inglestone Team who keep things running smoothly in my absence. Simon Apps for the super photography.
A special thank-you to the Head Teacher, Jon Allnutt, and to Beryl Booker at Fairford School, Gloucestershire, for all their help and for finding yet another team of excellent stitchers and advisers, without whom this book would not have been possible.
My school advisers were Steven Watson, Christopher Nash, Andrew Knight, Edward Bridges, Kate White, Harriet Hurdle, Rhys Hubbard-Miles, Rachael Goozee, Helen Taylor, Sarah Nicholls, Rebecca Sawyer, Joanna Shaw and Kiera Jones.
Thanks also to my faithful team of stitchers who stitch and check patterns, including Vera Greenoff, Hanne Castelo, Sarah Haines, Su Maddocks, Carol Lebez, Sophie Bartlett, Sarah Day, Jill Vaughan, Christine Banfield, Margaret Cornish, Sharon Griffiths, Barbara Webster, Suzanne Hunt and Jenny Kirby.
And finally, to DMC Creative World for the generous supplies of threads and fabrics, Tunley and Son for framing and art supplies, and Sarah Jane Gillespie for the clever decorative drawings.

index

Numbers in *italics* refer to Charts